REAL LIFE SEA MONSTERS

Great White Shark

by Ruth Owen

PowerKiDS press™

New York

Published in 2014 by The Rosen Publishing Group, Inc.
29 East 21st Street, New York, NY 10010

Produced for Rosen by Ruby Tuesday Books Ltd
Editor for Ruby Tuesday Books Ltd: Mark J. Sachner
US Editor: Joshua Shadowens
Designer: Emma Randall

Photo Credits:
Cover, 1, 4–5, 6–7, 8, 9 (top), 10–11, 14, 20, 25, 29 © Shutterstock; 9 (bottom) © C. Fallows, A.J. Gallagher, and N. Hammerschlag; 12–13, 15 © FLPA; 16–17, 18–19, 21, 26–27 © Superstock; 22–23 © Terry Goss.

Library of Congress Cataloging-in-Publication Data

Owen, Ruth, 1967–
 Great white shark / by Ruth Owen.
     pages cm. — (Real life sea monsters)
 Includes index.
 ISBN 978-1-4777-6249-3 (library) — ISBN 978-1-4777-6250-9 (pbk.) —
 ISBN 978-1-4777-6251-6 (6-pack)
 1. White shark—Juvenile literature. I. Title.
 QL638.95.L3O94 2014
 597.3'3—dc23

                              2013025766

Manufactured in the United States of America

CPSIA Compliance Information: Batch #W14PK7: For Further Information contact: Rosen Publishing, New York, New York at 1-800 237-9932

CONTENTS

SHARK!

For centuries, sailors told stories of sea serpents and giant beasts with tentacles that could pull a ship beneath the waves.

Today, we know these monsters do not exist. However, the world's oceans are home to many giant real-life hunters. Probably the best known of these are sharks.

Sharks have been on Earth for around 400 million years. As **carnivorous** dinosaurs stalked their **prey** on land, sharks hunted in the prehistoric seas. The dinosaurs are long gone, but sharks are still here, living and hunting in oceans around the world.

Without a doubt, the most feared shark is the great white. This powerful, skillful hunter is the world's largest **predatory** fish.

Great white sharks live in cool to warm oceans all over the world.

A great white shark

PHYSICAL FACTS

Great white sharks have been known to reach lengths of over 20 feet (6 m).

These huge **predators** usually weigh between 1,500 and 4,000 pounds (680–1,800 kg). Very large great whites, however, can weigh as much as 5,000 pounds (2,300 kg). That's as heavy as some SUVs!

Great whites have gray skin on the top halves of their bodies and white skin on their undersides. Like all sharks, they do not have a skeleton made of bones. A great white's skeleton is made of a tough, rubbery substance called **cartilage**. This is the same material in the hard, but bendy, parts of your ears.

Pectoral fin

Dorsal fin

Gray skin

Caudal fin

Eye

Nostril

White belly

Pectoral fin

Great white sharks get their name because of their size and their white bellies.

7

GREAT WHITE PREY

Great white sharks hunt and eat many different animals.

A great white's diet includes seals, sea lions, small whales, and dolphins. These sharks will also eat fish, squid, turtles, and even sea birds.

Many scientists believe that great white sharks are very smart animals. This idea makes a lot of sense. Ocean **mammals**, such as seals, sea lions, whales, and dolphins, are intelligent creatures. In order to catch these animals, a great white shark must be able to outsmart its meal!

Great whites don't only eat freshly caught meat. If a great white finds the carcass of a dead animal floating in the ocean, it will eat that, too.

A shark's-eye view of a sea lion

Dolphins

After a large meal, such as a seal, a great white shark can go for several weeks without eating.

Great white shark

Whale carcass

A PERFECT PREDATOR

A great white shark has powerful senses that help it detect its prey.

The shark's underwater vision is excellent, day or night. This is because the **retina** in each of its eyes is divided into two areas. One area is for seeing in bright daylight. The other area is for seeing in dark, nighttime waters.

If an animal is injured and bleeding, a great white can smell the blood in the ocean. In fact, it can smell the blood from 3 miles (5 km) away!

Great whites can also pick up tiny vibrations in water. An animal making the smallest of movements will quickly be detected by the shark, even if the animal is hundreds of feet (m) away.

A great white
can smell a drop
of blood in 25 gallons
(95 l) of
water.

THE ATTACK

Once a great white shark has detected its prey, the shark's speed and power make it a lethal killing machine.

Swimming just below the water's surface, a great white can approach its prey at speeds of 30 to 40 miles per hour (48–64 km/h). In the final seconds of its attack, it turns its head, so that its huge mouth is directly beneath the prey. Rising from the water, the great white attacks with a single killer bite.

As its victim bleeds to death, the shark waits. Finally, it moves in to eat its kill, biting off huge chunks and swallowing them without chewing.

The moment of attack

A great white shark's **streamlined**, torpedo-like shape allows it to move through water fast.

TEETH FOR TEARING

A great white shark's mouth can open nearly 4 feet (1.2 m) wide! When the shark's mouth opens, it is filled with truly terrifying teeth.

A great white shark may have up to 3,000 teeth in its mouth at one time. When it attacks its prey, the shark's bottom teeth **impale** the animal and hold it in place. Then the shark's top teeth tear into the animal's flesh. A great white shark's top teeth are serrated, which means the teeth have rough, sharp edges like the blade of a saw.

If one of the shark's teeth breaks off, it's not a problem. A replacement tooth will fill the gap so the shark's bite does not lose any of its power!

A great white shark's tooth

The teeth of a great white shark can grow to be more than 2.5 inches (6.4 cm) long!

A great white shark's mouth contains thousands of teeth.

THE ULTIMATE ATTACK

One moment a seal is swimming on the water's surface. The next, it is launched high into the air, clamped in the jaws of a great white.

It's a rare sight to see, but sometimes great whites attack by bursting out of the water. This type of giant, killer leap is known as breaching.

At high speed, the shark swims up from below its victim. Then, with perfect timing, it launches itself into the air, grabbing its prey at the same time. The power needed to propel a body weighing thousands of pounds (kg) out of the water is enormous.

The huge hunter twists and arches through the air before diving back into the ocean, carrying its victim to its death!

Great whites do not breach very often because this type of attack uses up huge amounts of energy.

FACE TO FACE

Would you go face to face with a great white shark? For some people, diving with sharks is a dream come true!

Shark watching tours allow people to watch sharks from a boat or dive with them. The **shark guide** attracts the animals to the boat by pouring a fishy, bloody mixture called "chum" into the water. Once a shark is attracted by the smell of the chum, a diver is lowered into the water inside a steel cage.

The smart shark seems interested to know what's in the cage. It swims back and forth, bumping the cage, just inches (cm) from the diver inside. Some divers even put their hands through the bars and touch a great white as it passes by!

The view from inside a shark diving cage.

A shark's skin looks smooth. In fact, it is so rough that it feels like sandpaper!

MEGALODON

The great white is the largest predatory shark in the ocean today. It would look small, however, compared to its giant prehistoric cousin, Megalodon.

This massive predator was longer than a school bus, reaching lengths of 60 feet (18 m). It weighed in at around 77 tons (69 t).

Megalodon hunted for whales and other large ocean creatures. Scientists think that to stay alive, each day, this huge, prehistoric shark needed to eat something the size of a modern-day great white shark!

For many years, scientists believed that great white sharks **evolved** from Megalodon. Recent investigations, however, show the prehistoric giant may be the **ancestor** of today's mako sharks.

Megalodon became **extinct** about 2 million years ago.

Megalodon tooth

21

LITTLE GREAT WHITES

A female great white is usually ready to mate and have young when she is 15 to 20 years old.

Baby sharks, called pups, grow in eggs inside their mother's body. Then they hatch from their eggs while still inside her body. Female great whites do not take care of their young. Once a mother shark gives birth, her pups swim away and are ready to start hunting for fish.

Each newborn pup is around 4 to 5 feet long (1.2–1.5 m). The shark pups may be fierce hunters, but until they grow bigger, they are in danger of being eaten by larger sea creatures. A pup might even become a meal for its own mother!

SHARK ATTACK?

Thanks to movies, like *Jaws*, many people believe great whites attack and kill people all the time. The truth is very different.

There have only been around 300 great white shark attacks on humans since people began keeping records. The sharks probably weren't deliberately attacking a person, though.

Many scientists believe that great whites are very curious animals. If they see something unusual in the water, they take a bite to find out if it might be good to eat. That's horribly unlucky for a person who is attacked, but the shark was only looking for food and acting naturally.

People should remember that when we go into the ocean, we are entering the shark's territory.

Scientists attract a great white with some food.

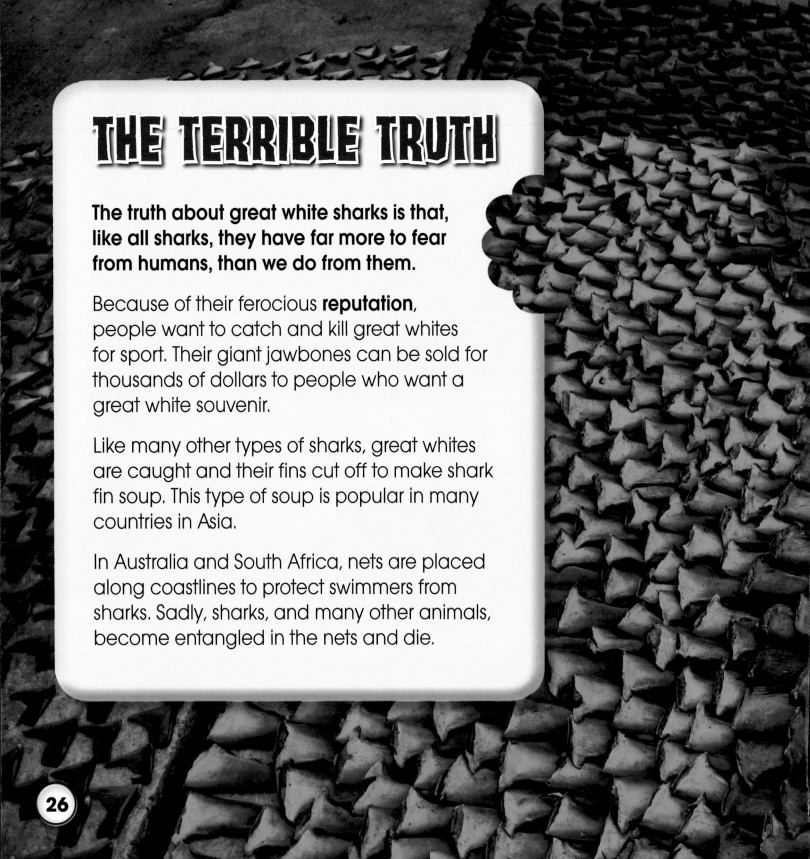

THE TERRIBLE TRUTH

The truth about great white sharks is that, like all sharks, they have far more to fear from humans, than we do from them.

Because of their ferocious **reputation**, people want to catch and kill great whites for sport. Their giant jawbones can be sold for thousands of dollars to people who want a great white souvenir.

Like many other types of sharks, great whites are caught and their fins cut off to make shark fin soup. This type of soup is popular in many countries in Asia.

In Australia and South Africa, nets are placed along coastlines to protect swimmers from sharks. Sadly, sharks, and many other animals, become entangled in the nets and die.

Shark fins

Every year, around 100 million sharks are killed by humans.

KEEPING IT REAL

A great white shark may be 15 to 20 years old before it breeds. Females only give birth to small numbers of pups at one time. This means that the number of great white sharks in the ocean goes up very slowly.

Great whites live in oceans around the world. So governments worldwide must protect them from hunting. Today, it is against the law to kill a great white shark in the oceans around many countries including South Africa, Australia, and New Zealand. More countries must put these types of laws in place, however.

Many types of sharks are now seriously **endangered**. If we want our oceans to be filled with beautiful real life sea monsters, sharks must be protected!

In China, Hong Kong, and Taiwan many people, including top chefs, are campaigning to stop people from eating shark fin soup.

GLOSSARY

ancestor (AN-ses-tur)
A relative who lived long ago.

breeds (BREEDZ)
Mates and has young.

carnivorous (kahr-NIH-vuh-rus)
Eating animals.

cartilage (KAR-tuh-lij)
Strong, rubbery tissue found in many areas of the body, including your nose and ears.

endangered (in-DAYN-jurd)
In danger of no longer existing.

evolved (ih-VOLVD)
Developed and changed gradually over many years.

extinct (ik-STINGKT)
No longer existing.

impale (im-PAYL)
To pierce with something pointed.

mammals (MA-mulz)
Warm-blooded animals that have a backbone and usually have hair, breathe air, and feed milk to their young.

predators (PREH-duh-turz)
Animals that hunt and kill other animals for food.

predatory (PREH-duh-tor-ee)
Living by hunting and eating other animals.

prey (PRAY)
An animal that is hunted by another animal as food.

reputation (reh-pyoo-TAY-shun)
A widely held belief about someone or something, often based on a particular kind of behavior. Many sharks have a reputation for being dangerous to humans.

retina (RET-in-uh)
The back of the eye that takes the light the eye receives and changes it into nerve signals so the brain can understand what the eye is seeing.

sea serpents (SEE SUR-pents)
Huge, ocean-dwelling monsters, which often have tentacles, that appear in old stories.

shark guide (SHARK GYD)
A person who is an expert on sharks, and takes visitors on boat trips to see sharks and learn about them.

streamlined (STREEM-lynd)
Shaped and built in a way that helps something move more quickly through the air or water; often pointed and smooth.

tentacles (TEN-tuh-kulz)
Long, arm-like body parts.

territory (TER-uh-tor-ee)
The area where an animal lives, finds its food, and finds partners for mating.

WEBSITES

Due to the changing nature of Internet links, PowerKids Press has developed an online list of websites related to the subject of this book. This site is updated regularly. Please use this link to access the list:

www.powerkidslinks.com/rlsm/sharks/

READ MORE

Coleman, Miriam. *Swimming with Sharks*. Flippers and Fins. New York: PowerKids Press, 2010.

Rake, Jody Sullivan. *Great White Shark*. Shark Zone. Mankato, MN: Capstone Press, 2011.

Reynolds, Hunter. *Hunting with Great White Sharks*. Animal Attack! New York: Gareth Stevens, 2013.

INDEX